THE CODE OF AYONIX

THIS BOOK BELONGS TO

_____

FOR KIDS WHO WANT TO BECOME EXPLORE

ISBN: 9798894582771

IN THE CYBER-CITY OF AYONIX, CEO DASH RAY RULED WITH WISDOM. HIS ELDEST SON, RAYN, A GENIUS IN AI AND ROBOTICS, WAS BELOVED BY ALL.

RAYN HAD THREE BROTHERS: LIAM, BARO, AND SHATRIK. TOGETHER, THEY TRAINED IN DIGITAL SECURITY, CYBER COMBAT AND FUTURISTIC WARFARE TO PROTECT AYONIX.

Dash Ray decided to step down and crown Rayn as the new leader. But his wife, Kiera, influenced by a hacked AI, opposed this decision.

UNDER AI MANIPULATION, KIERA DEMANDED THAT RAYN BE EXILED FOR 14 YEARS. HEARTBROKEN BUT LOYAL, RAYN LEFT WITH HIS WIFE SIENNA AND BROTHER LIAM.

THEY TRAVELED TO DANDAKA EXPANSE, A CYBERNETIC WASTELAND FILLED WITH ROGUE AI, DIGITAL OUTLAWS, AND BLACK-MARKET TECH DEALERS. RAYN USED HIS SKILLS TO SURVIVE.

ONE DAY, A HUMANOID DRONE NAMED SERAPHINA TRIED TO BREACH THEIR FIREWALL. LIAM QUICKLY CODED A SECURITY SHIELD, BLOCKING HER ATTACK.

Seraphina, furious, contacted her brother Ravex, the ruler of Lankatech, a floating AI-controlled metropolis. Ravex devised a plan to capture Sienna.

USING A STEALTH DRONE, RAVEX LURED SIENNA OUTSIDE THEIR ENCRYPTED ZONE. IN SECONDS, HIS PUSHPAK-9 HOVERCRAFT BEAMED HER AWAY TO LANKATECH.

SIENNA FOUND HERSELF TRAPPED IN TITAN TOWER, A FORTRESS OF DIGITAL FIREWALLS. RAVEX TRIED TO PERSUADE HER, BUT SHE REMAINED LOYAL TO RAYN.

Rayn and Liam sought help from Han-X, a humanoid AI with quantum computing skills and superhuman strength. Han-X agreed to aid them.

HAN-X ACTIVATED SKY-SCAN, A TRACKING PROGRAM, AND LOCATED SIENNA DEEP WITHIN LANKATECH. THE RESCUE MISSION WAS SET IN MOTION.

TO REACH LANKATECH, THEY BUILT A NEON BRIDGE ACROSS THE OCEANIC FIREWALL, HACKING THEIR WAY INTO THE ENEMY'S NETWORK.

RAVEX DEPLOYED ATTACK DRONES AND AI BOTS TO STOP THEM. RAYN, WIELDING HIS PHOTON SABER, FOUGHT THROUGH WAVES OF DIGITAL ENEMIES.

HAN-X INFILTRATED LANKATECH'S MAINFRAME AND SENT SIENNA A HOLOGRAPHIC MESSAGE: "RAYN IS COMING! HOLD ON!"

A FIERCE BATTLE ERUPTED. CYBER-SOLDIERS AND MECH WARRIORS TRIED TO STOP RAYN'S TEAM, BUT THEY ADVANCED USING CUTTING-EDGE WEAPONS AND HACKING SKILLS.

RAVEX, WITH HIS TEN AI-POWERED PROCESSORS, CALCULATED INFINITE BATTLE STRATEGIES. BUT RAYN'S DIVINE-TECH ALWAYS REMAINED A STEP AHEAD.

DURING THE BATTLE, LIAM WAS HIT BY A DARK ENERGY BLAST. HAN-X RUSHED TO RETRIEVE THE SANJEEVANI PATCH, A VITAL ANTIVIRUS PROGRAM.

WITH HIS SYSTEM REBOOTED, LIAM REJOINED THE FIGHT. THE FINAL SHOWDOWN BETWEEN RAYN AND RAVEX BEGAN—HUMAN INTELLIGENCE VERSUS AI SUPREMACY.

RAYN LAUNCHED HIS ULTIMATE ATTACK: DIVINE FIREWALL, A CODE SO POWERFUL IT SHUT DOWN RAVEX'S CORE SYSTEM, LEAVING HIM DEFENSELESS.

WITH A FINAL STRIKE, RAYN DELETED RAVEX'S CORRUPTED AI.
THE DIGITAL FORTRESS OF LANKATECH COLLAPSED, AND SIENNA WAS FREE.

THEY RETURNED TO AYONIX, GREETED BY MILLIONS IN A GRAND VIRTUAL CELEBRATION, MARKING THE END OF RAVEX'S DARK RULE.

AFTER 14 YEARS, RAYN RECLAIMED HIS RIGHTFUL PLACE AS LEADER OF AYONIX, ENSURING A FUTURE WHERE TECHNOLOGY SERVED HUMANITY, NOT CONTROLLED IT.

HAN-X CONTINUED TO UPGRADE SECURITY SYSTEMS,
ENSURING THAT NO DARK AI LIKE RAVEX WOULD EVER RISE AGAIN.

LIAM BECAME THE HEAD OF CYBER-DEFENSE, TRAINING THE NEXT GENERATION OF DIGITAL WARRIORS TO PROTECT THE WORLD.

BARO, RAYN'S YOUNGER BROTHER, LAUNCHED A PROJECT TO BUILD ETHICAL AI, PREVENTING MACHINES FROM EVER TURNING AGAINST HUMANS.

SHATRIK, ONCE RELUCTANT, NOW HELPED SPREAD AWARENESS ABOUT CYBER ETHICS, ENSURING PEOPLE USED TECHNOLOGY RESPONSIBLY.

SIENNA, A BRILLIANT SCIENTIST, DEVELOPED AI-POWERED MEDICAL BOTS TO HEAL PEOPLE AND MAKE HEALTHCARE ACCESSIBLE TO ALL.

WITH RAYN'S LEADERSHIP, AYONIX FLOURISHED INTO THE MOST ADVANCED YET ETHICAL CYBER-CITY, WHERE TECHNOLOGY AND MORALITY COEXISTED.

THE CODE OF AYONIX WAS WRITTEN, ENSURING THAT AI WOULD NEVER SURPASS
HUMAN WISDOM, KEEPING POWER IN RESPONSIBLE HANDS.

RAYN AND SIENNA RULED WITH FAIRNESS,
ENSURING THE BALANCE BETWEEN PROGRESS AND HUMANITY REMAINED STRONG.

THE PEOPLE OF AYONIX THRIVED, LIVING IN A FUTURE WHERE INNOVATION AND ETHICS SHAPED A BETTER TOMORROW.

EVEN AFTER CENTURIES, LEGENDS OF RAYN AND HIS CYBER-WARRIORS WERE PASSED DOWN, INSPIRING FUTURE GENERATIONS.
MORAL OF THE STORY:
GOOD ALWAYS PREVAILS OVER EVIL, AND TRUE LEADERSHIP IS ABOUT USING POWER FOR THE GREATER GOOD.

IN THE END, COURAGE, LOYALTY, AND RIGHTEOUSNESS ALWAYS TRIUMPHED—EVEN IN THE AGE OF ARTIFICIAL INTELLIGENCE.